HENDERSON'S
WHOLEFOOD
COOKBOOK

Henderson's Wholefood Cookbook

Illustrations by
Tim Archbold

Northern Books
from Famedram

ISBN 0-905489-57-8

Northern Books from Famedram, Ellon AB41 9EA   www.northernbooks.co.uk
Printed by Thomson Press (I) Ltd, C-35, Phase-II, Noida

Contents

Conversion Tables

The following tables are the approximate conversions for metric and imperial measures used throughout this book. All are approximate conversions, which have either been rounded up or down. It is important not to mix metric and imperial measures, stick to one system or the other.

WEIGHTS		VOLUME	
$^1/_2$oz	15g	1 fl oz	25ml
1oz	25g	2 fl oz	50ml
2oz	50g	3 fl oz	75ml
3oz	75g	5 fl oz ($^1/_4$ pint)	150ml
4oz	110g	10 fl oz ($^1/_2$ pint)	275ml
5oz	150g	15 fl oz ($^3/_4$ pint)	400ml
6oz	175g	1 pint	570ml
7oz	200g	$1^1/_4$ pints	700ml
8oz	225g	$1^1/_2$ pints	900ml
9oz	250g	$1^3/_4$ pints	1 litre
10oz	275g	2 pints	1.1 litres
11oz	310g	$2^1/_4$ pints	1.3 litres
12oz	350g	$2^1/_2$ pints	1.4 litres
13oz	375g	3 pints	1.75 litres
14oz	400g	$3^1/_4$ pints	1.8 litres
15oz	425g	$3^1/_2$ pints	2 litres
1lb	450g	$3^3/_4$ pints	2.1 litres
$1^1/_4$lb	550g	4 pints	2.3 litres
$1^1/_2$lb	700g	5 pints	2.8 litres
2lb	900g	6 pints	3.4 litres
3lb	1.4kg	7 pints	4 litres
4lb	1.8kg	8 pints	4.5 litres
5lb	2.3kg		

MEASUREMENTS

$^1/_4$in	$^1/_2$cm
$^1/_2$in	1cm
1in	2$^1/_2$cm
2in	5cm
3in	7$^1/_2$cm
4in	10cm
6in	15cm
7in	18cm
8in	20$^1/_2$cm
9in	23cm
10in	25$^1/_2$cm
11in	28cm
12in	30$^1/_2$cm

OVEN TEMPERATURES

275°F	140°C	Gas Mark 1
300°F	150°C	Gas Mark 2
325°F	170°C	Gas Mark 3
350°F	180°C	Gas Mark 4
375°F	190°C	Gas Mark 5
400°F	200°C	Gas Mark 6
425°F	220°C	Gas Mark 7
450°F	230°C	Gas Mark 8
475°F	240°C	Gas Mark 9

Foreword

OUR AIMS at Henderson's today vary little from those of Janet Henderson to whom we dedicate this book. Her vision, beliefs and commitment encouraged a healthy approach to eating well ahead of its time. Many years later we are still producing quality vegetarian food using the finest ingredients available.

Served in a relaxed and informal but appealing way, it continues to follow the recipe invented by Janet for Henderson's success.

For years fans of Henderson's food have been begging that we disclose the secrets behind Henderson's salads, desserts, hot dishes and breads. After a mere 35 years perfecting the recipes we can now proudly present *Henderson's Wholefood Cookbook*.

On the pages that follow you will find a collection of recipes ranging from original old favourites to recently introduced ones which are equally as popular. Try them at home and enjoy the taste of Henderson's.

NICHOLAS HENDERSON
DECEMBER 1998

Henderson's founder, Janet Henderson, left,
in discussion with an assistant in the Salad Table
from an early 60s newspaper shot.

Henderson's
Wholefood
Cookbook

Where it all started: Henderson's Shop and beneath it
the Salad Table in Edinburgh's Hanover Street.

Introduction

LIKE ARTHUR'S Seat and The Mound in Edinburgh, Henderson's just seems to have been there forever. It is difficult to imagine Hanover Street without it.

In fact it was the shop above the famous Salad Table restaurant that got there first. Henderson's founder Janet Henderson opened the shop in 1962 as an outlet for the bountiful natural food that was flowing from the family farm in East Lothian.

Janet Henderson was quite a character. Born in 1913 into a solidly middle class Glasgow family, she early on distinguished herself as someone who liked to do things her own way. As a young woman she travelled widely in Europe and developed a taste for progressive European ideas.

One special area of interest was diet. She was much taken with the wholefood approach to eating and returned from her studies on the Continent a confirmed vegetarian. It was no surprise therefore that when she married into an East Lothian farming family her influence should begin to show with her husband, the rugby playing 'Mac' Henderson.

From a mixed farming operation Spitalrigg, where they lived, became ever more devoted to Janet Henderson's wholefood ideals. Bringing seven strapping children into the world caused only a minor diversion from the main task and by the mid-fifties when the youngest, Oliver, had started school she was ready to take her organic ideas a stage further.

Produce from the farm found its way into the kitchens of parents of her childrens' friends and on to the shelves of local shops. The family Ford Consul groaned under the weight of the fresh produce it was made to carry and soon had to be replaced by a second hand Bedford van which, when not being raced around the fields by the high spirited children, ferried the produce into town.

In 1961 Janet Henderson borrowed the money to open a shop in Hanover Street. At last there was an outlet for the wholesome produce being grown on the farm.

Managing Partner Nicholas Henderson recalls that busy though she was, his mother still managed to make time for family holidays. A couple of years before the shop opened he remembers a Youth Hostelling holiday which took him aged 11, sister Sara aged 15, Danielle aged 12 and his mother, then aged 45, round the North of Scotland – she on a "pushbike with no gears" covering formidable distances each day.

Business in the shop was brisk and a couple of years later, in 1963, the derelict basement beneath the shop was done up and turned into a restaurant. Henderson's famous Salad Table restaurant was born.

At first the fare was relatively simple, as was the decor. When in year two a table licence was applied for questions were asked as to how a "self service restaurant whose customers sat on orange boxes could possibly merit a licence." But Henderson's got one and the customers loved it.

Hendersons rapidly became an institution. At Festival time the queue for the food counter often spilled right up the stone steps and out on to the street. But the founding philosophy of good food at sensible prices still ruled, as it does to this day.

The business grew organically, in line with the product. A bakery dedicated to Henderson's brown loaves and rolls opened in separate premises in Canonmills in 1964. Five years later Henderson's Bistro in Thistle Street opened its doors for the first time.

In the formative days much of the culinary inspiration came from Janet Henderson's prime helper, a Spanish cook by the name of Covadonga who had an inspired way with vegetables, a favourite dish being her Bravastouriana.

In 1973, following an illness picked up on a journey to the Far East, Janet Henderson died aged just 60. Though it had lost its founding force, Janet Henderson's personality had impressed itself so strongly on the institution that bears the family name that it continued to flourish under the continuing control of that family.

Over the years Henderson's has remained ever faithful to the founding philosophy, serving only wholesome natural food in a burgeoning variety of attractive forms and always at reasonable prices.

The recipes that have formed the core of the Henderson menu have often been passed on by word of mouth in the kitchen, with new dishes being added and old ones being refined. Until the publication of this book many of them had never been committed to paper.

If you enjoy turning these recipes into real dishes remember you can always compare your own results with the originals in Henderson's Salad Table, still in its original premises in Hanover Street and the Henderson's Bistro in Thistle Street, both in Edinburgh, or by buying one of the growing range of Henderson's widely available pre-cooked convenience dishes.

The spirit that founded the enterprise has not changed: now perhaps it will inspire an even wider audience.

Vegetable Stock

5 litres (8³/₄ pints) water
1 large carrot
2 bouquet garni
1 savoy cabbage leaf
2 bay leaves

1 medium onion
½ a leek
½ head celery
salt and pepper

Roughly chop vegetables, boil all ingredients in water for approximately two hours or until all the vegetables are very well cooked. Strain through sieve and use as required. You can use any vegetable to make your stock.

Yellow Split Pea Soup

SERVES 4-6

250g (¹/₂lb) yellow split peas
1 clove garlic
1 large onion
salt and pepper

1 tbspn caraway seeds
2 litres (3 pints) vegetable stock
110g (4oz) carrots
1 tbspn vegetable oil

Sauté onions, garlic and caraway seeds for five minutes in oil.
Slice carrots, wash the split peas thoroughly and add to onions
etc. Lightly sauté for a few minutes then add stock and bring to
the boil. Simmer until split peas are soft enough, season to taste
and serve.

Original Vegetable Soup

SERVES 6-8

2 onions (diced)
1 bay leaf
1 tbspn mixed herbs
¹/₄ or 1 small turnip (diced)
2.3 litres (4 pints) vegetable stock
salt and pepper

4 courgettes (diced)
1 small head celery (diced)
4 medium carrots (diced)
oil for frying

Sauté onion, mixed herbs, salt, pepper and bay leaf in little
vegetable oil until onions are transparent. Add carrots and
turnip and sauté for another 10 minutes before adding the rest
of your vegetables and stock (if not enough stock make some
up with bouillon paste). Cook until vegetables still holding
together and season to taste. Could also add fresh kale,
broccoli, cauliflower or other ends of vegetables.

Carrot Soup

SERVES 4-6

1 medium onion
2 medium potatoes
2 tbspns oil
1.4 litres (2½ pints) vegetable stock
1 pinch caraway seeds (ground)

6 good size carrots
1 cup double cream
salt and pepper

Chop onions and sauté in oil until softened. Grate carrots and potatoes and add them to the onion together with caraway seeds. Add vegetable stock and bring to the boil then reduce heat and simmer until carrots and potatoes are cooked. Liquidise or push through a sieve, add double cream and heat gently. Season to taste and serve.

Minestrone Soup

SERVES 4-6

1 small onion	1 small carrot
1 small potato	2 sticks celery
1 small yellow pepper	1 small green pepper
1 small courgette	¼ cup pasta shells
1 savoy cabbage leaf	3 cups chopped tomatoes
1 clove garlic	2 tbspns fresh basil
2 tbspns oil	½ cup red wine (optional)
2 tbspns tomato purée	2 tbspns cornflour
1 litre (1¾ pints) vegetable stock	¼ cup pasta shells

Finely chop the onions and dice all the other vegetables (into 1cm pieces). Sauté onions with oil and garlic, add diced vegetables and basil then sauté for a further five minutes. Add all other liquid and tomato purée, bring to the boil and add pasta. Simmer until pasta is al dente, 10-12 minutes. Mix cornflour with water and add to the soup to thicken. Season to taste and serve.

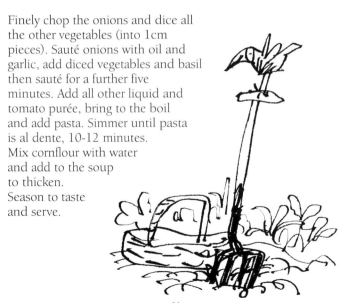

Tomato and Sorrel Soup

400g (14oz) plum tomatoes
2 tbspns oil
1 tbspn tarragon
salt and pepper

1 large onion, finely chopped
1 bunch sorrel leaves
150ml ($^1/_4$ pint) dry white wine
400ml ($^3/_4$ pint) vegetable stock

Gently sauté onion in oil, add wine and bring to the boil to evaporate the alcohol. Reduce heat and add tomatoes, sorrel and stock then simmer for 20 minutes. Salt and pepper to taste, add tarragon and serve.

Cauliflower and Blue Cheese Soup

25g (1oz) butter
570ml (1 pint) milk
$^1/_4$ pint double cream
fresh chopped parsley
275ml ($^1/_2$ pint) vegetable stock

1 medium onion
cornflour
110g (4oz) Stilton
salt and pepper
1 large cauliflower

Sauté onion in butter, add cauliflower florets and sauté for a further three minutes, making sure the cauliflower does not brown. Add stock and milk then heat gently until the cauliflower is just softening. Crumble Stilton into the soup and add double cream and chopped parsley. Thicken with a little cornflour and water if necessary, season to taste and serve.

Spicy Parsnip Soup

6 good size parsnips
4 medium potatoes
1 medium onion
1 cup double cream
salt and pepper
400ml (³/₄ pint) vegetable stock

2 tbspns oil
1 medium carrot
pinch ground coriander
pinch of chilli powder
pinch ground cumin

Peel and grate parsnips, carrots and potatoes and finely chop the onion. Sauté onion and spices in oil until soft, add grated parsnips, carrot and potatoes. Add stock and bring to the boil, reduce heat and simmer until all the vegetables are cooked. Liquidise or pass through a sieve, add double cream and season to taste.

The spicier you want the soup the more chilli you add!

Curried Almond Soup

SERVES 4-6

25g (1oz) butter
2 tbspn mild curry powder
900ml (1¹/₂ pints) vegetable stock
4 tbspns toasted flaked almonds

1 large onion, finely chopped
110g (4oz) ground almonds
salt and pepper
fresh coriander

Sauté onions in butter until soft, add curry powder and cook for another two minutes. Add stock and ground almonds, bring to the boil and simmer for approximately 10-15 minutes. Allow to cool slightly and liquidise or pass through a sieve. Return to the heat and add chopped coriander and seasoning. Garnish with toasted flaked almonds and serve.

Tomato and Tarragon Soup

SERVES 4-6

25g (1oz) butter
225g (8oz) plum tomatoes
4 large tomatoes, chopped
salt and pepper
2 tbspns chopped fresh tarragon

1 onion, finely chopped
570ml (1 pint) tomato juice
150ml (¹/₄ pint) double cream
1 clove garlic crushed

Sauté garlic and onion in butter until soft, add chopped tomatoes and tomato juice. Bring to the boil and simmer for approximately 15-20 minutes, add chopped fresh tomatoes and tarragon and cook for a further 10 minutes. Season to taste and add double cream just before serving.

Courgette and Mushroom

SERVES 4

2 medium courgettes
2 medium tomatoes
$^1/_4$ cup Henderson's French Dressing

1 cup mushrooms
25g (1oz) fresh dill

Halve courgette lengthways and thinly slice, slice mushrooms and cut tomatoes into eight. Roughly chop dill and toss everything together along with French Dressing and serve.

Egg, Cheese and Breadcrumb (mock crab)

SERVES 4

2 hard boiled eggs
$^1/_2$ cup grated red Cheddar
$^1/_2$ cup yogurt

2 cups wholemeal breadcrumbs
$^1/_2$ cup milk
$^1/_2$ cup mayonnaise

Finely chop eggs and mix with breadcrumbs and grated cheese. Fold in yogurt and mayonnaise, gradually add milk until a soft, moist consistency is achieved. Top with toasted breadcrumbs and serve. Any Cheddar can be used depending on personal preference, the more mature the cheese, the stronger the flavour.

Curried Noodle

¼ cup raisins
½ small red pepper
½ small yellow pepper
1 cup mayonnaise
225g (8oz) dried egg noodle (soaked for one hour)

2 small tomatoes
½ small green pepper
1 small courgette
1 tbspn curry powder

Slice peppers and courgettes and quarter the tomatoes. Place noodles and vegetables in a bowl with raisins. Mix curry powder and mayonnaise (you may wish to add more curry powder to taste) and fold this into the noodle mix. Place salad in a serving bowl and garnish with fresh coriander or flaked almonds.

Carrot, Cheese and Watercress

SERVES 4-6
2 medium carrots
1½ cup grated white Cheddar
1 small onion
2 medium tomatoes
½ bunch watercress

Grate carrots and cheese, thinly slice onion and cut tomatoes into eights. Roughly chop watercress, mix all ingredients and serve.

Tomato, Basil and Feta Tartlets

MAKES 24
225g (8oz) plain flour
pinch salt
175g (6oz) butter
50ml (2fl oz) water

FILLING
6 medium tomatoes
small bunch fresh basil
110g (4oz) feta cheese
black olives stoned (garnish)

Sieve flour and salt into a bowl then rub in the butter until mixture resembles breadcrumbs. Pour in half the water and mix together then gradually add the rest of the water to make a dough. Roll out dough to 3mm (^{1}/8 in) thick and cut into 24 circles. Press into tartlet tins, prick pastry cases and bake in a preheated moderate oven for 15-20 minutes or until slightly brown. Place on a wire rack to cool.

Filling – finely chop tomatoes and basil, mix and season lightly. Place some of the mix in each tartlet and crumble some feta cheese on top. Garnish with sliced olives and serve.

Any size/shape of tartlets can be made.

Celery, Apple and Hazelnut

SERVES 4-6

1 good size head of celery
3 red apples
½ cup hazelnuts
¼ cup mayonnaise
½ cup yogurt
½ lemon

Finely slice celery, core
and dice apples and
sprinkle with a little
lemon juice. Mix everything
together and serve.

Beansprout, Ginger and Brazil Nuts

Serves 4-6

1 bag beansprouts
$^1/_2$ small yellow pepper
$^1/_2$ cup Brazil nuts
1 small tomato
1 small carrot

$^1/_2$ small red pepper
$^1/_2$ small green pepper
1 tbspn steamed ginger
1 bunch watercress

Grate carrot, roughly chop Brazil nuts, cut tomato into eight and slice peppers. Mix everything together and serve.

Beetroot and Mustard Dressing

SERVES 4

6 large beetroots

2 medium tomatoes

HENDERSON'S MUSTARD DRESSING

3-6 tbspns sunflower oil
1 tbspn cider vinegar
1 tspn French mustard
1 tspn grain mustard
salt and paper to taste

Cook the beetroot by boiling
in water, this will take around
one hour. When cold, peel and grate the beetroot and finely
slice tomatoes. Mix together, top with Henderson's Mustard
Dressing and serve.

Banana, Cucumber and Cashew Nuts

SERVES 4

1 large cucumber
1 cup sour cream
$^1/_2$ cup broken cashew nuts (unsalted)

2 large bananas
juice from $^1/_2$ lemon

Roast cashew nuts in oven until golden brown and allow to
cool. Cube the cucumber and slice bananas then sprinkle with
lemon juice. Mix all ingredients together and serve.

Fennel, Cheese and Dill

Serves 4

2 medium heads fennel
3 medium tomatoes
1/4 cup Henderson's French Dressing

1 cup cubed red Cheddar
2-3 sprigs fresh dill

French Dressing

3-6 tbspns sunflower oil
1 tbspn cider vinegar
salt and pepper to taste

1 tspn French mustard
pinch of mixed herbs

Roasted Vegetable

Serves 4

1 medium onion
1 medium tomato
1 medium green pepper
1 pack baby corn
1/4 cup olive oil
salt and pepper

1 medium courgette
1 medium red pepper
1 cup mushrooms
1/2 small aubergine
1 clove garlic
chopped fresh basil

Dice all the vegetables and toss in olive oil, basil and crushed garlic. Season and bake in the oven for approximately 20 minutes 200°C (400°F/Gas Mark 6). Serve hot or cold

Mushroom Pâté

SERVES 4-6

110g (4oz) soft low-fat cheese
pinch of tarragon
salt and pepper

450g (1lb) mushrooms
25g (1oz) margarine

Wash mushrooms and put through the grater blade of a food
processor. Put into a pan with tarragon and margarine and cook
until soft. Allow to cool and
mix thoroughly with soft
cheese.

Season to taste
and garnish with a
slice of mushroom
and parsley.

Hummus

SERVES 4-6

400g (14oz) chickpeas (and juice) 4 cloves garlic, crushed
2 tbspns tahini   1 tbspn lemon juice
salt and pepper   olive oil

Liquidise all ingredients except chickpea juice and olive oil.
Gradually add liquid until a smooth consistency is achieved
(you may not need it all). Salt and pepper to taste.

*Individual taste of hummus can vary, add more or less garlic and/
or lemon juice as required.*

Three Cheese Tzatziki

500g (1lb 2oz) cream cheese   1 cucumber finely chopped
50g (2oz) strong red Cheddar   50g (2oz) Danish blue cheese
4 cloves garlic, crushed   ground pepper

Mix cream cheese, grated Cheddar and crushed garlic together,
add diced cucumber and crumbled blue cheese. Season with
ground pepper to taste.

Ideal to serve with sliced apple and tortilla chips.

Baked Nut and Red Wine Pâté

2 cloves garlic
1 small onion finely chopped
1 tspn paprika
1/4 pint vegetable stock
1 small tin chestnut pureé
2 eggs

50g (2oz) butter
1/2 head celery finely chopped
1 tspn fresh basil
1/4 pint red wine
50g (2oz) breadcrumbs
1 tspn soya sauce

Sauté onions, spices and garlic in butter until soft, add chopped celery and sauté for a further two to three minutes. Add wine and stock and bring to the boil. Remove from the heat and add all your other ingredients, blend slightly still leaving a coarse texture. Place the mixture in an ovenproof dish and bake at 180°C (325°F/Gas Mark 4) until the mixture is firm to touch (approximately 3/4 hours). Once cool serve with oatcakes or wholemeal bread.

Guacamole

4 ripe avocados
1 lemon
4 cloves garlic

2 medium tomatoes
1 small onion
salt and pepper to taste

Squeeze juice from lemons and place in a bowl. Peel and stone avocados and add to the bowl with crushed garlic. Liquidise or mash to a pulp. Add finely diced onion and tomatoes, mix well and season. Garnish with a slice of lemon and parsley.

Henderson's Béchamel Sauce

660ml (1 pint) milk
1/4 cup flour (sieved)
salt and pepper

1/2 cup vegetable oil
1 tspn English Mustard

Heat oil in a thick saucepan and add the flour and mustard to make a roux. Remove from heat and gradually stir in the milk mixing well until smooth. Return to heat and stir continually bringing back to the boil. Simmer for two minutes and season with salt and pepper.

Henderson's Cheese Sauce

MAKES 800MLS (1 1/2 PINTS)
660mls (1 1/4 pints) milk
1/4 cup plain flour
1 cup strong mature Cheddar
1 small onion, chopped

1/2 cup oil
1 tspn English Mustard
salt and pepper
1 bay leaf and some cloves

Mix oil and flour to make a roux, cook for 2-3 minutes and set aside. Place onion, cloves and bay leaf in the milk and gently warm to allow flavours to infuse. Discard onion, bay leaf and cloves and gradually add milk to the roux, stirring well until sauce forms. Add mustard, cheese and seasoning.

Broccoli and Brie Crumble

SERVES 4

4 heads broccoli
1 medium onion
25g (1oz) margarine
300mls ($^{1}/_{2}$ pint) milk

150g (5oz) mixed peppers
2 tomatoes
35g (1$^{1}/_{2}$oz) flour
50g (2oz) Brie

TOPPING

25g (1oz) almonds
50g (2oz) cashew nuts
25g (1oz) margarine

50g (2oz) hazelnuts
75g (3oz) oats
25g (1oz) sunflower seeds

Chop up and cook the broccoli, drain and put to one side.
Sauté onions and peppers then add flour and some milk to
make a roux. Slowly add the rest of the milk, stirring well, and
add broccoli to the sauce. Chop and add tomatoes and Brie
then season to taste.

Topping – melt margarine and add roughly chopped nuts,
oats and sunflower seeds. Mix thoroughly and spread on top of
broccoli mixture. Bake for $^{3}/_{4}$ hour until golden brown on top.

Stuffed Aubergine with Wild Mushroom Sauce

2 large aubergines
150g (5oz) carrots (grated)
30g (1½oz) toasted oatmeal
5 tbspns tamari
2 tbspns sunflower oil
4 tbspns toasted nuts (crushed) cashews, Brazil nuts, hazelnuts

150g (5oz) onions (chopped)
150g (5oz) courgette (grated)
2 cloves garlic
2 tbspns fresh sage
salt and pepper

SAUCE

150g (5oz) wild mushrooms
2 tbspns fresh tarragon
50g (2oz) butter
dash of wine

75g (3oz) onions (chopped)
50g (2oz) flour
450mls (¾ pint) milk
salt and pepper

Halve the aubergine lengthways and bake at 150°C (300°F/Gas Mark 2) for 10 minutes. Remove from the oven and allow to cool. Sauté onion, sage and garlic until onions are soft, add carrots and tamari and sauté for a further three to four minutes mixing well. Add courgettes, crushed nuts and oats, mix well and cook for a further five minutes on medium heat and season to taste. Scoop out flesh from aubergine pieces and fill with the mixture.

   Sauce – sauté onions and tarragon in some vegetable oil until soft and gradually add flour to make a roux. Add milk stirring continuously and cook for two to three minutes on a low heat. Slice the wild mushrooms and add to your sauce with a dash of wine. Season to taste.

Broccoli with Mustard and Tomato Sauces

SERVES 4-6
3 or 4 heads broccoli (trimmed)

TOMATO SAUCE

1 onion (finely chopped)	6 tomatoes (quartered)
1 clove garlic	1 dtspn sunflower oil
1 tin chopped tomatoes	chopped fresh basil
salt and pepper	1 bay leaf

MUSTARD SAUCE

50g (2oz) margarine	25g (1oz) white flour
25g (1oz) brown flour	300ml (1/2 pint) soya milk
salt and pepper	mustard (to taste)

Cut broccoli into florets and soak in salt water for one hour then blanch and chill until sauces are ready.

Tomato sauce – sauté onions in oil, add bay leaf, basil and fresh tomatoes and sauté for a further five minutes. Add tinned tomatoes and seasoning.

Mustard sauce – melt margarine in saucepan and add flour to make a roux. Gradually add soya milk until the sauce is correct consistency and add seasoning and coarse grained mustard.

Put a ladle of tomato sauce into the bottom of a baking tray. Arrange broccoli florets and cover completely with alternate diagonal stripes of tomato sauce and mustard sauce. Heat through and serve.

Nut Loaf with Oriental Sauce

SERVES 8

150mls (¼ pint) vegetable stock
25g (1oz) sesame seed
75g (3oz) wholemeal breadcrumbs
125g (4½oz) crunchy peanut butter
150g (5oz) finely diced onion
2 tspns mixed herbs
salt and pepper to taste

25g (1oz) pumpkin seed
150g (5oz) grated hazelnuts
100g (3½oz) grated cashew nuts
450g (1lb) wholemeal puff pastry
4 tbspns natural tamari
3 cloves garlic
1 tbspn chopped parsley

ORIENTAL SAUCE

15g (½ oz) fresh ginger
1 tspn Chinese 5-spice
75g (3oz) finely sliced onion
salt and pepper
½ packet baby corn
2 tbspns cornflour

2 cloves garlic
1 tbspn olive oil
50g (2oz) finely sliced peppers
50g (2oz) beansprouts
150ml (¼ pint) natural tamari
900ml (1½ pints) vegetable stock

Nut Loaf – place all ingredients (except stock) into mixing bowl and mix well, gradually add stock until the mixture is moist. Roll out pastry to approximately 20cm x 20cm and place mixture along the centre making a log shape. Wet pastry with a little soya milk and wrap into a parcel folding in each end. Brush the top with some milk and sprinkle with a little sesame seeds. Bake at 150°C (300°F/Gas Mark 2) for one hour.

Sauce – fry garlic, ginger, onion, green pepper and 5-spice for a few minutes. Add stock and tamari, simmer for 10 minutes, add baby corn and simmer for a further 3-4 minutes. A few minutes before serving add beansprouts and thicken with cornflour if necessary.

Suggested vegetables – parsnips, carrots and Brussels sprouts. Ideal as an alternative Christmas lunch.

Spinach and Cashew Nut Lasagne

SERVES 4 - 6

900g (2lbs) spinach
salt, pepper and nutmeg
9 sheets lasagne verdi
50g (2oz) vegetarian Parmesan

25g (1oz) margarine
100g (4oz) cashew nuts
100g (4oz) grated cheese

CHEESE SAUCE

50g (2oz) margarine
570ml (1 pint) milk
75g (3oz) grated Cheddar

50g (2oz) wholemeal flour
salt and pepper

Preheat oven to 190°C (375°F/Gas Mark 5). Cut any large spinach leaves then cook and squeeze dry.

Cheese sauce – melt margarine and gradually add the flour to make a roux. Add milk slowly, stirring continuously until smooth consistency is achieved. Add grated cheese and salt and pepper to taste.

To make up (makes one lasagne 30cm x 23cm) – pour one third of cheese sauce into the bottom of a lasagne dish and place three pasta sheets on top. Spread out half the spinach evenly and sprinkle with some cashew nuts. Add a layer of grated cheese, three more sheets of pasta and pour over another third of cheese sauce. Distribute remainder of the spinach and add grated cheese. Cover with remaining pasta and finish with the rest of your sauce. Sprinkle with Parmesan and cashew nuts then bake for 30 minutes until golden brown.

Spinach Tian

Serves 4-6

450g (1lb) spinach
225g (8oz) Cheddar cheese
225g (8oz) mixed peppers
125g (4½oz) mushrooms
salt and pepper
1 small glass dry white wine (optional)

225g (5oz) rice
6 eggs
225g (8oz) onions
4 cloves garlic
pinch of nutmeg

Cook rice as per instructions. Shred spinach and sauté in a little margarine, add nutmeg and some seasoning then set aside. Finely chop onions and sauté with crushed garlic and nutmeg. Add peppers, mushrooms and cook until al dente. Mix with spinach, cooked rice and grated cheese. Mix in beaten eggs, salt and pepper, and white wine if used. Bake in an ovenproof dish at 200°C (400°F/Gas Mark 6) until firm and golden brown.

Vegetable Lasagne

SERVES 4-6

12 sheets lasagne verdi
300g (11oz) carrot
300g (11oz) mushroom
1 medium green pepper

300g (11oz) courgettes
300g (11oz) turnip
1 medium red pepper
2 medium onions

TOMATO SAUCE

2 tbspns vegetable oil
2 medium yellow peppers
250ml (1/2 pint) tomato juice
1/2 tspn dried basil

2 medium green peppers
2 medium onions
700g (11/2lbs) tinned tomatoes
1/2 tspn dried oregano

TOPPING

2 medium red peppers
2 medium onions
200g (7oz) margarine
150g (5oz) cheese
salt and pepper

2 medium green peppers
100g (4oz) flour
1.2 litres (21/4 pints) milk
1 tspn mixed herbs

Tomato Sauce – slice peppers and onion. Lightly sauté onions in oil with basil and oregano, add peppers and sauté for a further five minutes. Add tinned tomatoes and tomato juice.

Topping – slice peppers and onion, sauté in margarine for five minutes and add herbs. Add flour to make a roux then, adding milk gradually, make creamy sauce with cheese and seasoning. Once everything is ready grease a lasagne dish and begin with four sheets of lasagne. Spoon over half the tomato sauce, steamed vegetables a thin layer of topping sauce. Cover with another four sheets of lasagne and repeat until lasagne is finished. Finish with surplus topping and garnish with parsley and a little grated cheese. Bake for 45 minutes at 220°C (425°F/Gas Mark 7).

Vegetable Strudel

SERVES 4-6

4 courgettes (diced)	4 large carrots (diced)
4 onions (diced)	250g (9oz) mushrooms
1 head broccoli florets	2 tbspns margarine
275ml ($^1/_2$ pint) soya milk	2 tbspns flour
9 sheets filo pastry	

Sauté onions with mixed herbs and bay leaf, add carrots and cook until al dente. Separate filo pastry sheet and cover with a damp cloth. Once the carrots are cooked add courgettes and then peppers. Blanch broccoli separately. Mix all vegetables together and leave for five minutes. Whisk flour and soya milk, add to the vegetables stirring well and cook for five minutes. Season to taste.

Lightly grease a baking tray and lay three pastry sheets in the bottom. Add the filling and cover with another six or seven sheets. Lightly grease on top and cut into portions *before* cooking.

You can add any other sort of vegetables to this dish, baby corn, green beans, turnip etc.

48

Henderson's Vegetarian Haggis with Clapshot

SERVES 4

75g (3oz) mushrooms (finely chopped)
75g (3oz) brown lentils (soaked for two to three hours)
50g (2oz) pinhead oatmeal (soaked for one hour)
50g (2oz) red kidney beans (soaked, cooked and chopped)
25g (1oz) margarine
150g (5oz) carrots (grated)
2 garlic cloves (finely chopped)
1 tspn garam masala
freshly ground sea salt
150g (5oz) onions (chopped)
1 tbspn tamari/soya sauce
1 tbspn vegetable oil
$1/2$ level tspn freshly ground black pepper

Prepare vegetables and pulses in advance, using a food processor will speed up the process. Sauté garlic, onion and seasoning with a little oil until soft.

Add brown lentils and carrot and simmer on a low heat until lentils are soft, stirring to prevent sticking. The moisture content of the soaked lentils and carrot should be sufficient, but if not add a very small amount of vegetable stock or water. Add mushrooms and allow to soften before adding kidney beans. Stir in margarine and more black pepper to taste. Finally add oatmeal (drained and rinsed) and mix well, the oatmeal should retain its texture.

Serve with clapshot – 2lb potatoes and one medium turnip boiled and mashed, add a knob of butter and season to taste.

Moussaka

Serves 4-6

1 cup kidney beans (dried) or 1 tin kidney beans

1 large onion	2 tbspns sunflower oil
250g (9oz) potatoes	1 large aubergine
2 large tomatoes	1 tbspn paprika
1 tspn cinnamon	1 egg
4 cups puréed tomatoes	$^{1}/_{2}$ cup red wine
1 tbspn tomato purée	$^{1}/_{4}$ cup yogurt

200ml (8 fl oz) Henderson's Béchamel Sauce

If using dried kidney beans soak overnight, boil in water until cooked (approximately one hour), drain and rinse. Prepare tinned beans as per instructions. Thinly slice the onions and sauté until soft, add paprika and cinnamon then sauté for a further two to three minutes. Add sliced potatoes, red wine, tinned tomatoes, tomato purée, bring to the boil and simmer gently until potatoes are cooked (approximately 30 minutes). Add cooked kidney beans, heat through and season to taste.

Slice tomatoes and aubergine, lightly sauté the aubergine and drain off any excess oil. Layer half the tomatoes and cooked aubergine slices in the bottom of an ovenproof dish. Cover with potato and kidney bean mix and top with another layer of tomatoes and aubergine.

Finally, mix the cheese sauce with yogurt and an egg. This is the topping for your moussaka. Pour over tomato and aubergine layer and place in a oven 220°C (425°F/Gas Mark 7) for about 20 minutes or until golden brown.

Potato and Mushroom Goulash

SERVES 4-6

25g (1oz) butter	800g (1¾lb) potatoes
400g (14oz) mushrooms	1 medium onion
1 tspn caraway seeds	1 clove garlic
½ cup vinegar	½ cup red wine
3 cups stock	½ cup sour cream
1½ tbspns cornflour	salt and pepper
1 tbspn tomato purée	1 dspn paprika

Finely dice onion and dice potatoes into chunky pieces. Sauté onions and garlic in butter until transparent, add ground caraway seeds and paprika and cook for a further minute. Add potatoes, red wine and vinegar, cover and simmer until potatoes are almost cooked. Roast mushrooms in a moderate oven and add to potatoes. Add tomato purée, mix well and thicken slightly with cornflour if required. Season to taste and garnish with sour cream.

Vegetable Satay

SERVES 4

1 cup mushrooms
1 small red pepper
1 small aubergine
1 pack baby corn
1 cup soya milk
1 cup fresh orange juice
2 cloves garlic
1 tbspn cornflour
$^1/_2$ cup crunchy peanut butter (unsalted)

2 medium carrots
1 small green pepper
1 medium courgette
1 small bunch French beans
2 cups tomato juice
$^1/_4$ cup vinegar
1 fresh chilli
1 tbspn soya sauce

Halve mushrooms, babycorn and French beans, peel and slice carrots and dice the other vegetables. Place everything on a large baking tray with a little vegetable oil and roast in the oven 230°C (450°F/Gas Mark 8) until al dente.

Crush garlic and finely chop the chilli, sauté together in a little oil, add soya milk, tomato juice, vinegar, soya sauce and peanut butter. Bring to the boil making sure the peanut butter has melted and thicken with cornflour if required. Season to taste. Add roasted vegetables to the sauce and serve with rice or noodles.

Broccoli and Cauliflower Harlequin

SERVES 4

3 cups passata (puréed tomatoes)
800ml (1½ pints) cheese sauce
2 heads broccoli
¼ cup red lentils (soaked)
¼ tspn chilli
¼ tspn coriander
2 tbspns oil

1 small onion
1 small cauliflower
1 clove garlic
1 medium tomato
¼ tspn cumin
1 tbspn tomato purée
1 tspn cornflour

Grated cheese and wholemeal breadcrumbs for topping

Lentil Base – finely chop the onion and sauté with garlic, chilli, cumin and coriander until soft. Add the soaked lentils, passata and tomato purée and bring to the boil. Allow to simmer gently for 15-20 minutes, stirring occasionally, until the lentils are cooked and no more. Chop up tomato and add to the lentil mix, thicken with cornflour if required and season to taste.

While the lentils are cooking prepare cauliflower and broccoli by cutting into bite size florets. Slightly undercook the florets as this dish will be reheated before serving. Drain off any excess water and place to one side.

Pour lentil mix into an ovenproof casserole dish, spread cooked florets evenly over the top and cover with cheese sauce. Finally sprinkle with the grated cheese and wholemeal breadcrumbs. Bake in the oven 220°C (425°F/Gas Mark 7) for approximately 20 minutes until golden brown.

Leek and Potato Pie

SERVES 4

4 good sized leeks
200g (7oz) baby potatoes
400ml (¾ pint) cheese sauce

4 medium tomatoes
1 cup grated red Cheddar
2 tbspns sunflower oil

Boil potatoes, clean and slice leeks and tomatoes. Sauté leeks in oil until soft. Make up a cheese sauce and mix with cooked leeks. Pour mixture in an ovenproof casserole dish and top with tomato and sliced potatoes. Finish with some grated cheese and bake in a hot oven 230°C (450°F/Gas Mark 8) until cheese is bubbling and the dish is heated through.

Leek Croustade

SERVES 4-6

4 good size leeks	1 medium onion
1 cup mushrooms	2 medium tomatoes
$1/4$ cup sunflower oil	$3/4$ cup flour
570ml ($1^1/2$ pint) milk	

BASE

$1/2$ cup red Cheddar	3 tbspns sunflower oil
salt and pepper	2 cups wholemeal breadcrumbs

Base – mix all ingredients and press firmly into an ovenproof dish, bake in a hot oven until golden brown.

Wash and slice leeks, halve the mushrooms, roughly chop onions and quarter the tomatoes. Sauté leeks and mushrooms and set to one side. Sauté onions in oil until soft and add flour to make a roux. Gradually add the milk stirring continuously until sauce is formed. Reduce heat and add leeks, mushrooms and chopped tomatoes. Pour into base and bake in a moderate oven until golden brown.

Cheese and Herb Shortbread

SERVES 6-8

200g (7oz) plain flour

150g (5oz) butter

2 tbspns double cream

25g (1oz) Danish blue cheese or strong Cheddar

25g (1oz) cornflour

25g (1oz) Parmesan

2 tbspns mixed herbs

Mix together all ingredients until a smooth dough is formed. Grease and line a flan dish and press the dough into it. Prick the surface with a fork, mark sections and bake at 150°C (300°F/Gas Mark 2) for 40 minutes until golden brown. Cut sections while still hot.

Sugar Free Apricot Slice

400g (14oz) apricots (soaked in 400ml water)
200g (7oz) vegetable margarine
140g (5oz) malt extract
400g (14oz) oats
200g (7oz) organic wholemeal flour
40g (1½oz) coconut

Melt margarine and malt extract gently, add oats and flour and divide in two. Spread one half into a greased flan tin and press down firmly. Combine apricots and water until they form a rough paste and spread over the base. Take second half of mixture and add coconut, mix together and spread evenly on top of the apricots and press gently. Bake at 180°C (350°F/Gas Mark 4) for approximately 20 minutes until golden brown. Once cool cut into small wedges and serve.

Sugar Free Banana Bar

400g (14oz) peeled bananas
140g (5oz) cashew nuts
140g (5oz) oats
15g (¹/₂oz) cinnamon

180ml (6 fl oz) sunflower oil
140g (5oz) coconut
140g (5oz) raisins
15g (¹/₂oz) nutmeg

Mix bananas and oil until smooth, add the other ingredients and mix lightly until bound together. Press into a greased flan dish and bake at 180°C (350°F/Gas Mark 4) for approximately 15 minutes or until golden brown. Cut into small wedges once cool.

Spiced Carrot Cake

2 eggs
60ml (2$^{1}/_{2}$ fl oz) sunflower oil
40g (1$^{1}/_{2}$oz) currants
$^{1}/_{2}$ tspn nutmeg
85g (3$^{1}/_{2}$oz) organic soft flour

85g (3$^{1}/_{2}$oz) sugar
40g (1$^{1}/_{2}$oz) coconut
1 tspn cinnamon
100g (4 oz) grated carrots
1 tspn baking powder

Beat eggs, sugar and oil together until thoroughly mixed and add flour, baking powder and spices. Fold in currants, cocunut and grated carrots and pour into a greased loaf tin. Bake at 180°C (350°F/Gas Mark 4) for approximately 45 minutes or until cooked.

Oatcakes

680g (1½lb) organic bread flour
285g pinhead oatmeal
12g (½oz) baking powder
50ml (2 fl oz) water

110g (4oz) organic soft flour
225g (8oz) vegetable margarine
20g salt

Mix all dry ingredients and add water in stages until a dough is formed. Leave to rest for around 15 minutes. Roll out to approximately 2mm (depth of 10p) and cut into rounds, makes approximately 50. Place on a greased baking tray and bake at 190°C (375°C/Gas Mark 5) for 15-18 minutes.

Apple and Cinnamon Tea Loaf

2 eggs
50g (2oz) vegetable margarine
285g (10¹/₂oz) soft flour
¹/₂ tspn bicarbonate of soda
1 tspn cinnamon
75g (3oz) raisins
200ml (7 fl oz) milk

250g (9oz) chopped apples
160g (5¹/₂oz) sugar
2 tspns baking powder
¹/₂ tspn salt
¹/₂ tspn nutmeg
50g (2oz) chopped walnuts

Lightly beat egg, add apple, margarine, sugar. Fold in sieved flour, bicarbonate of soda, baking powder and spices until mixture is smooth, do not beat. Fold in the raisins and walnuts and pour into a greased loaf tin. Bake at 180°C (350°F/Gas Mark 4) for approximately one hour. Allow to stand for 10 minutes before turning onto baking tray to cool.

Sunflower and Honey Loaf

550g (1¼lb) wholemeal flour
pinch salt
35g (1¼oz) sunflower seeds
25g (1oz) sunflower oil

1 tbspn fresh yeast
½ tbspn clear honey
320ml (12 fl oz) warm water

Mix all ingredients except water which is added in steps until a dough is formed. Knead for approximately 20 minutes and place in a warm area to rise. After one hour knead for a further 20 minutes and transfer to two loaf fins or form into a chosen shape. Sprinkle the top with some sunflower seeds and leave in a warm place for another hour until twice original size. Bake at 250°C (500°F/Gas Mark 10) for approximately 25 minutes.

Milk Loaf

500g (1lb 2oz) strong bread flour (untreated white)
1/4 tbspn sugar   pinch salt
1/2 tbspn sunflower oil   1 tbspn milk powder
1 tbspn fresh yeast   340ml (12 fl oz) warm water
1 egg

Mix all ingredients except water which is added in steps until a dough is formed. Knead for approximately 20 minutes and place in a warm area to rise. After one hour knead for a further 20 minutes and transfer to two loaf fins or form into a chosen shape. Sprinkle the top with some sunflower seeds and leave in a warm place for another hour until twice original size. Bake at 250°C (500°F/Gas Mark 10) for approximately 25 minutes.

Fresh and Dried Fruit with Sour Cream

SERVES 4-6

'1 'tart' apple (eg Granny Smith)   275ml (¹/2 pint) sour cream
425g (15oz) dried fruit   200g (7oz) fresh fruit
110g (4oz) stem ginger shavings in syrup (drained)

Chop up fresh fruit, grapes are good for colour, and mix with
the dried fruit (pre-soaked), add ginger shavings and stir in
some of the sour cream. Top with the rest of the sour cream,
sprinkle with ginger and serve.

Fruit Crumble

Almost any fruit can be used – depending on what's in season

CRUMBLE TOPPING

900g (2lb) fruit – apples, raspberries, rhubarb etc
110g (4oz) wholemeal flour   75g (3oz) butter
50g (2oz) brown sugar

Prepare the fruit and place in an ovenproof dish – you may
require a little extra sugar to sweeten. Put flour, butter and
sugar in a bowl and work them to crumbs with your fingers.
Sprinkle over the top of your chosen fruit and bake in a
moderate oven until crisp and golden brown. A few sesame or
sunflower seeds can be added to the topping for a nuttier
texture.

Banana and Tofu Cheesecake

MAKES 1

1¹/₂ blocks tofu
1 orange
175g (6oz) creamed coconut
450g (1lb) bananas

1 flan case
1 small lemon
75g (3oz) raisins

TOPPING

4 bananas
1 tbsp of orange juice

25g (1oz) coconut

Mash tofu and bananas in a bowl with finely grated orange and lemon rind and their juice. Add all other ingredients, mix well and divide between two flan cases, pressing down firmly. Bake for approximately 30 minutes at 150°C (300°F/Gas Mark 4) until golden brown and leave to cool. Slice banana thinly into some orange juice and arrange over flan. Sprinkle with coconut and serve.

Chocolate and Hazelnut Torte

450g (1lb) nuts (finely grated)
225g (1lb) butter or margarine
225g (1/2lb) breadcrumbs

800g (1 3/4lbs) soft brown sugar
1/2 tspn baking powder
10 eggs (size 1)

Whisk eggs and sugar until stiff and slowly add melted butter/margarine and baking powder. Fold in wholemeal breadcrumbs and nuts and pour into baking tray (lined with greaseproof paper). Bake in a moderate oven until golden brown. Allow to cool and cut the sponge into layers.

Mix fresh cream and chocolate sauce and layer through the sponge. Decorate top with cream and sauce. Alternatively purée soft fruits and layer through sponge with cream and decorate the top with fruits and cream.

This recipe is very vague because it is a recipe that has been passed down over many years and is done from mind rather than 'by the book'. I hope you are able to make the torte for your friends but our chefs advise that it is very difficult to work with the sponge when baked. It is very fragile and they would not recommend attempting to make it into any shape other than round or square.

Chocolate Mousse

SERVES 4

3 eggs
175g (6oz) dark chocolate
1 tspn coffee

25g (1oz) soft brown sugar
100ml (4 fl oz) double cream

PIPING

50ml (2 fl oz) double cream

25g (1oz) chocolate

Melt the chocolate and separate eggs. Whisk the egg yolks with sugar until stiff and pale in colour. Set to one side. In a different bowl whisk egg whites until stiff and forming peaks then gently fold into the yolk mix. Mix melted chocolate with double cream and coffee. Add this to the whipped egg folding gently and encouraging as much air into the mix as possible. The colour should be a light brown throughout.

Pour mix into individual ramekin dishes and place in the fridge to set for at least six hours, preferably overnight. To decorate, pipe whipped cream on top of mousse and sprinkle with some grated chocolate

For orange and chocolate mousse, add two tbspns Cointreau; mint and chocolate mousse add two tbspns Créme de Menthe; almond and Amaretto mousse, add one tbspn ground almonds and one tbspn Amaretto.

Fruit Fools

1 cup fresh fruit purée (raspberries, strawberries, mango,
   blackberries, rhubarb, passion fruit etc)

2 cups natural yogurt   2 cups double cream

1 tspn honey   6 small sprigs mint

Purée some fruit of your choice. Whisk cream, yogurt and
honey along with a tablespoon of fruit purée until forming
peaks. Divide the rest of the fruit purée into glasses and spoon
over yogurt and cream mixture. Decorate with a sprig of fresh
mint and a piece of the fruit of your choice.

Lemon Tart

SERVES 6

BASE

150g (5oz) butter
110g (4oz) icing sugar
50g (2oz) ground almonds

310g (11oz) plain flour
2 eggs

FILLING

2 lemons
150ml (¼ pint) double cream

4 eggs
150g (5oz) caster sugar

Cream butter and icing sugar. Add eggs and ground almonds then gradually add flour until a soft dough is formed. Chill for one hour and line a loose bottom flan dish with the pastry. Grate lemon rind and squeeze juice from both lemons. Gently beat the eggs, don't froth, and add cream, sugar, lemon juice and rind. Pour into the pastry base and bake in oven at 200°C (400°F/Gas Mark 6) until firm to touch but not browning, approximately 30-45 minutes.

Muesli

3 firm eating apples
1 unwaxed lemon
125g (4½oz) rolled oats
50ml (2 fl oz) double cream

1 unwaxed orange
50g (2oz) chopped hazelnuts
100ml (4 fl oz) yogurt
50g (2oz) raisins

Grate apple and a little orange and lemon rind. Peel and finely chop the lemon and orange and mix all ingredients. Serve topped with toasted nuts and sweeten with honey if required.

Fresh Fruit Salad

1 grapefruit
1 Granny Smith apple
1 kiwi fruit
1 pear
$^1/_4$ small pineapple

1 red apple (Gala)
1 banana
1 small bunch black grapes
$^1/_4$ small melon
570ml (1 pint) fresh orange juice

Roughly chop the fruit, place in a bowl and pour over orange juice, chill and serve.

For exotic variation add mango, papaya, starfruit, fresh apricot and nectarine.

Cheesecake

350g ($^3/_4$lb) soft cheese
350g ($^3/_4$lb) biscuit crumbs
2 tbspns honey

275ml ($^1/_2$ pint) cream
110g (4oz) butter
fruit flavour (from puréed fruit)

Melt butter, add biscuit crumbs and press into plastic tray and leave to cool. Mix the rest of the ingredients in a bowl until soft and fluffy and spread over your biscuit base. Decorate with appropriate fruit and serve.

Vacherin

1 dozen fresh meringues
1 measure Cointreau
275ml (¹/₂ pint) double cream

2 medium oranges
¹/₂ cup stem ginger in syrup

Peel and segment one orange. Whip up double cream until slightly stiff and put some of it aside for garnish. Mix the rest of the cream with Cointreau, ginger, most of the orange segments and half the meringues (broken up). Place in a serving bowl and top with the remaining meringues and piped cream. Garnish with some orange slices and mint sprigs.

Passion Fruit Brûlée

Serves 8-10

8 passion fruits
150ml (¹/₄ pint) sour cream
2 tspns almond liqueur (or essence)

150ml (¹/₄ pint) double cream
1 dtspn icing sugar

Scoop out passion fruit flesh and place in a bowl (sieve flesh if you prefer not to have stones). Whip cream until it starts to thicken and fold in sour cream, almond liqueur and icing sugar.

To serve – divide into heat-proof ramekins and liberally sprinkle with demerara sugar. Place under a hot grill until the sugar melts and has formed a toffee-like crust.

Walnut and Strawberry Shortcake

175g (6oz) plain flour
75g (3oz) soft brown sugar
110g (4oz) butter
110g (4oz) walnuts
2 tbspns icing sugar
450g (1lb) strawberries, hulled and chopped
275ml (¹/₂ pint) double or whipping cream

Grind walnuts in a food processor or crush with a rolling pin.
Cream butter and caster sugar, add nuts and gradually add the
flour until a dough is formed. Roll out the dough to
approximately 1cm thick and cut into biscuit rounds or heart
shapes with a pastry cutter. Bake at 190°C (375°F/Gas Mark 5)
until golden brown (15-20 minutes), leaving to harden before
removing from baking tray.

Whip up cream and fold in icing sugar and chopped
strawberries. Place some of the mix in between two shortbread
biscuits, dust with icing sugar and serve.

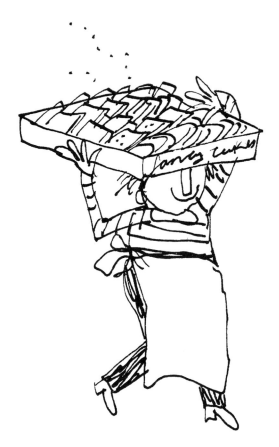

Florentine Cake

SERVES 8-10

100ml (4 fl oz) milk
250g (9oz) icing sugar
200g (7oz) flaked almonds
350g (12oz) mixed peel/raisins/sultanas

200g (7oz) butter
110g (4oz) plain flour
275g (10oz) dark chocolate

Melt butter and icing sugar and add all other ingredients except the chocolate. Divide into two lined flan dishes and bake at a low heat 150°C (300°F/Gas Mark 2) until lightly browned on top, 35-40 minutes. Once cool melt the chocolate and cover top of the cake. Can be made into individual cakes if desired.

Plum Compôte

SERVES 4

Halve 2lb plums and place in saucepan with 150ml water, to stop them from sticking, a little sugar to taste and one cap of vanilla essence. Cook for 5-10 minutes stirring often and taste for sweetness. Place in a bowl and allow to cool overnight.

Fruit Trifle

2 cups fresh fruit salad *(see recipe p74)*
2 tbspns mixed fruit jam
200ml (7 fl oz) custard

570ml (1 pint) double cream
1 measure sherry

SPONGE

2 eggs
65g (2¹/₂oz) Dove organic flour

65g (2¹/₂oz) caster sugar
¹/₄ tspn baking powder

Whisk eggs until they are double in volume and a pale colour. Fold in sugar and sieved flour and pour into a lined baking tin. Bake in moderate oven for 15 minutes until golden brown and allow to cool. Roughly grate.

Mix fruit salad and 1 tbspn of the jam (keeping ¹/₄ of the mix aside for decorating) and place in the bottom of a medium-sized glass bowl. Mix the grated sponge with tbspn jam, fruit salad and sherry. Cover with custard and refrigerate until custard is set.

When ready to serve cover with whipped cream and decorate with remaining fruit mixture.